PHYLLIS'S *Favorite* RECIPES

PHYLLIS'S *Favorite* RECIPES

PHYLLIS TAYLOR

Rev. date: 12/11/2025

To order additional copies of this book, contact:
Xlibris
844-714-8691
www.Xlibris.com
Orders@Xlibris.com
749750

Table of Contents

<u>Cooking Tips</u>

- Read entire recipe before beginning to cook.

- Seasonings and Spices - Add or delete according to your taste.

- Use glass measuring cup to measure liquids.

- When measuring brown sugar, lightly pack brown sugar to get a more accurate measurement.

- Before baking a cake, allow butter and eggs to warm to room temperature.

- Bake cakes in center of oven.

- Allow cake to cool 20 minutes then remove from pan to avoid cake sticking to pan.

- To make a boxed cake taste like a homemade cake add 1 cup of all-purpose flour, ½ c sugar, 1 tsp of baking powder, ½ c softened butter and 2 tsp of vanilla flavor to boxed cake mix ingredients.

- For perfect pastry pie crust, mix together 1 egg and a 2 tsp of water. Brush crust with egg mixture. This keeps the bottom of crust from getting soggy.

- For perfect graham cracker crust, mix together 1 egg white and a 2 tsp of water. Brush crust with egg mixture. Bake at 350 degrees for approx. 5 minutes or until slightly brown. This keeps crust from getting soggy.

- For fluffy and lightly scrambled eggs, add a pinch of baking powder and small amount of milk (add amount of baking powder and milk based on number of eggs).

- When baking a dish that requires liquid, gradually adjust the amount of liquid you pour into the mix to avoid adding too much liquid. You can always add more liquid in but you can't take liquid out.

- When cooking, cook the items that take the longest amount of time to cook first.

Gumbo

1 c chopped onion
1 c chopped bell pepper
½ c chopped red bell pepper
½ c chopped yellow bell pepper
¼ c chopped green onion
1 chopped celery stalk (optional)
½ lb okra (optional)
2 chopped garlic cloves
¼ c butter
½ c flour
4 c chicken broth
3 c water
1 lb chopped smoked sausage
1 deboned rotisserie chicken
1½ lb peeled and deveined shrimp
1 Tbsp Creole seasoning
½ tsp seasoning salt
1 tsp garlic powder
½ tsp paprika
½ tsp black pepper
¼-½ tsp red pepper
3 tsp filé
2 bay leaves

Prep and pre-measure ingredients to save time. In large pot add butter and flour. Cook until flour is brown. Add seasonings. Sauté and add vegetables. Sear and add smoked sausage. Add chicken broth, water and rotisserie chicken. Add filé and bay leaves. Simmer 45 minutes. Add shrimp (seafood). Bring to boil then reduce heat. Simmer 15 more minutes. Serve over rice.

Optional: Add 1 lb crab legs, 1 c crabmeat, and/or 1 c oysters.

Red Beans

2 c kidney beans
1 c chopped onions
½ c chopped bell peppers
1 chopped garlic clove
1 Tbsp vegetable oil
2 c chopped smoked sausage
3 c chicken broth
2 tsp Cajun seasoning
¼ tsp black pepper
½ tsp garlic powder
¼ tsp cayenne pepper
1 bay leaf

Soak beans in water for approx. 4 hours. Drain. In large pot, add all ingredients. Cook on low heat for 1 hour and 45 minutes or until beans are slightly tender. Add water if needed. Serve over rice.

Beef Tips

1 lb beef tips
2 Tbsp vegetable oil
1 c chopped onions
1c chopped bell peppers
2 chopped garlic cloves
2 chopped green onions
2 tsp Creole seasoning
½ tsp garlic powder
¼ tsp black pepper
Dash of cayenne pepper
2 bay leaves
2 c chicken broth
1 c water
¼ tsp vinegar

Flour Mixture
2 Tbsp flour
½ c water

Drizzle vegetable oil into pot. Add beef tips. Sear beef tips until brown. Add and sauté onions, bell peppers, garlic, green onions and bay leaves. Add seasonings. Add chicken broth, water and vinegar. Bring to boil. Reduce heat. Cook 1 hour or until beef tips are tender. In small bowl stir together 2 Tbsp flour and ½ c water. Add to beef tips. Bring beef tips to boil, then reduce heat and simmer for 10 minutes or until gravy thickens. Serve over rice or mashed potatoes.

Meat Loaf

1 lb ground beef
1 - 8 oz can tomato sauce
1 egg
½ c chopped onions
½ chopped bell peppers
12 crushed crackers
1 tsp Creole seasoning
½ tsp garlic powder
¼ tsp black pepper

Mix all ingredients together. Shape into meatloaf. Place on baking dish/pan.

Meat Loaf Sauce

1 - 8 oz can tomato sauce
2 Tbsp brown sugar
2 Tbsp vinegar
2 tsp mustard
1 ½ c water
Season to taste

Mix all ingredients together. Pour sauce over meatloaf. Bake at 350 degrees for 45 minutes.

Southern Fried Chicken

Milk Mixture

1 c milk or buttermilk
2 tsp Cajun seasoning
1 egg (optional)
2 Tbsp flour

Flour Coating

2 c flour
2 tsp Cajun seasoning
¼ tsp black pepper
½ tsp paprika
¼ tsp cayenne pepper
½ tsp garlic powder
1 tsp baking powder

Milk mixture: Combine milk, seasoning, egg and flour in a bowl.

Flour Coating: Add flour ingredients in plastic bag and shake.

Dip chicken pieces in milk mixture, place pieces in plastic bag, and shake to coat chicken. Repeat dipping and shaking process for double coating. Heat oil in cast iron skillet or deep fryer on medium heat, reduce heat if necessary. Place chicken in oil and fry approx.. 15 minutes or until golden brown on each side. Remove from oil.

Homemade Brown Gravy

2 Tbsp flour
2 Tbsp vegetable oil
¼ c chopped onions
¼ chopped bell peppers
¼ c green onions
1 chopped garlic clove
½ tsp Creole seasoning
¼ tsp garlic powder
¼ tsp black pepper
1 c chicken broth
1 c water

Sauté 2 Tbsp vegetable oil, onions, bell pepper, green onions, garlic, Creole seasoning, garlic powder, and black pepper in skillet. Add flour and brown. Add chicken broth and water. Bring to boil. Reduce heat. Simmer until gravy thickens. Stir occasionally.

Chicken Spaghetti Casserole

(Follow Fried Chicken Recipe or Use favorite
already prepared Fried Chicken)
8 pieces of chicken
12 oz spaghetti cooked and drained
1 jar/can favorite spaghetti sauce
½ c chopped onions
½ c chopped bell peppers
1 tsp Italian seasoning
2 tsp Creole seasoning
1 tsp garlic powder
¼ tsp black pepper
¼ tsp paprika
1 crushed bay leaf
2 Tbsp sugar (optional)
¾ c water
2 c shredded sharp cheddar cheese (optional)

Mix spaghetti sauce, onions, bell peppers, seasonings, garlic powder, paprika, bay leaf, sugar (optional) and water. Add cooked spaghetti. Toss ingredients together. Bring to a boil, then simmer for 15 minutes. Place chicken in greased pan/ dish. Pour spaghettis over chicken. Bake at 375 degrees for 25 minutes or until cheese is golden brown.

Glazed Ham

28 oz pkg fully cooked thick sliced ham
1 c pineapple juice
½ c brown sugar

Preheat oven to 400 degrees. Mix together pineapple juice and brown sugar. Place ham in pan. Pour pineapple mixture over ham. Garnish with sliced pineapples. Cover ham with foil. Cook 20 minutes. Remove ham from oven. Leave ham covered with foil until ready to serve.

Peachy Pork Chops

4 Pork Chops
2 tsp Cajun seasoning
¼ tsp black pepper
¼ tsp garlic powder
2 Tbsp vegetable oil
½ c water
1-29 oz can peaches
¼ c brown sugar

Season pork chops with Cajun seasoning, black pepper, and garlic powder. In large skillet heat vegetable oil. Brown pork chops on each side. Add peaches, brown sugar and water. Bring to boil. Reduce heat. Simmer pork chops for 20 minutes or until pork chops are tender. Serve over rice.

Fried Shrimp

25-30 large deveined shrimps
Vegetable Oil

Milk Mixture

1 egg
1 c milk
2 Tbsp flour

Flour Mixture

½ tsp Cajun seasoning
¼ tsp garlic powder
¼ tsp black pepper
2 c shrimp fry
½ c chicken fry
¼ teaspoon baking powder

Heat vegetable oil in deep fryer or skillet. Mix together egg, milk and flour in a bowl. Mix seasoning, garlic powder and black pepper, baking powder, shrimp fry and chicken fry together in a bowl. Dip shrimp in mild mixture then coat with shrimp fry mixture. Shake off excess. Fry until golden brown.

Fried Fish

4 Fish Filets
Vegetable Oil

Milk Mixture

1 egg
1 c milk
2 Tbsp flour

Flour Mixture

½ tsp Cajun seasoning
¼ tsp garlic powder
¼ tsp black pepper
2 c fish fry
¼ c chicken fry
¼ teaspoon baking powder

Heat vegetable oil in deep fryer or skillet. Mix together egg, milk and flour in a bowl. Mix seasoning, garlic powder and black pepper, baking powder, fish fry and chicken fry together in a bowl. Dip shrimp in milk mixture then coat with fish fry mixture. Shake off excess. Fry until golden brown.

Homemade Battered Fries

2 lg sliced potatoes
Vegetable Oil

Milk Mixture

1 egg
1 c milk
3 Tbsp flour
½ tsp Cajun seasoning

Flour Mixture

2 c flour
2 ½ tsp Cajun seasoning
½ tsp garlic powder
¼ tsp black pepper
¼ tsp baking powder

Heat vegetable oil in deep fryer or skillet. Mix egg, milk, 3 Tbsp flour and ½ tsp seasoning in a bowl. Mix 2 c flour, 2 tsp seasoning, garlic powder, pepper and baking powder in a bowl. Dip potatoes in milk mixture then coat with flour mixture. Shake off excess flour. Fry until golden brown.

Baked Beans

2 - 15oz cans pork n beans
1 lb cooked ground beef
½ c chopped smoked sausage
2 Tbsp vegetable oil
1 c cooked bacon or real bacon bits
1 c chopped onions
½ c chopped bell peppers
1 chopped garlic clove
½ c BBQ Sauce
½ c brown sugar
1 Tbsp mustard
¼ c water
1 tsp Creole seasoning
½ tsp garlic powder
¼ tsp black pepper

Cook 2-3 slices of bacon, then crumble or use 1 cup of real bacon bits. Brown ground beef and smoked sausage. Drain. Pour vegetable oil in skillet. Sauté onion, bell pepper and garlic. Add pork n beans, cooked ground beef, smoked sausage, bacon or bacon bits, BBQ sauce, brown sugar, mustard and water. Add seasoning, garlic powder and black pepper. Pour into greased baking dish. Bake at 375 degree for 30-35 minutes.

<u>Greens</u>

2 smoked turkey wings

2 bunches of collard greens, peeled and washed

2 c chicken broth

1 c chopped onions

1 c chopped bell peppers

¼ c chopped green onion

2 chopped garlic gloves

2 bay leaves

4 tsp Cajun seasoning

¼ tsp cayenne pepper

½ tsp garlic powder

¼ tsp black pepper

3-4 c water (cover greens)

2 Tbsp vegetable oil

2 Tbsp butter (optional)

2 Tbsp sugar (optional)

Add all ingredients to pot, bring to boil and reduce heat. Cook on low for 1½-2 hours or until tender.

Macaroni and Cheese

1 box macaroni and cheese
Cheese sauce package
1 - 12 oz can evaporated milk
2 c shredded sharp cheddar
¼ c butter
2 eggs, beaten
2 tsp Creole seasoning
¼ tsp garlic powder
¼ tsp black pepper

Cook macaroni as directed on package. Drain. Mix macaroni, cheese sauce packet, butter, evaporated milk, cheese, eggs, seasoning, garlic powder and pepper. Pour into greased casserole baking dish. Top with shredded cheese. Bake at 375 degrees for 35-45 minutes or until bubbly and golden brown.

Cornbread

1 c yellow corn meal
½ c all-purpose flour
2 tsp baking powder
½ tsp salt
1 c milk
¼ c vegetable oil
2 Tbsp sugar (optional)

Preheat oven to 400 degrees. Pour oil in pan/skillet. Heat pan/skillet in oven for approx. 10-15 minutes or until oil is hot. While pan/skillet is heating combine corn meal, flour, baking powder, sugar & salt. Add milk and oil. Mix until ingredients are combined. Pour mixture into heated pan/skillet. Bake for 25 minutes, until golden brown.

Fried Cornbread

1 c yellow corn meal
¾ boiling water
¼ tsp baking powder
¼ tsp salt

Heat skillet or deep fryer on medium heat until oil is hot. While oil is heating combine corn meal, baking powder & salt. Add boiling water and mix ingredients together. Wait a few minutes to allow mixture to cool. Spoon mixture into hand and flatten to desired thickness. Drop into cooking oil. Cook until golden brown on each side.

Cornbread Dressing

Cornbread

1 pkg Mexican cornbread
1 c yellow cornmeal
¼ c flour
2 tsp baking powder
1 Tbsp sugar (optional)
½ c chopped onions
½ c chopped bell peppers
½ c diced celery (optional)
1 tsp Creole seasoning
¼ tsp garlic powder
¼ tsp black pepper
1 egg
1 c milk
¼ c vegetable oil

Preheat oven to 400 degrees. Pour ¼ c oil in pan/skillet. Heat pan/skillet in oven for approx. 10-15 minutes or until oil is hot. While pan/skillet is heating combine Mexican cornbread, cornmeal, flour, baking powder, sugar, onion, bell pepper, seasoning, black pepper and garlic powder. Add egg and milk. Mix until ingredients are combined, about 1 minute. Pour mixture into heated pan/skillet. Bake for 25 minutes, until golden brown.

Dressing

Cornbread
2 c chicken broth
½ c milk
¼ c butter
1½ tsp Creole seasoning
¼ tsp black pepper
¼ tsp garlic powder

In large bowl crumble cornbread. Add chicken broth, butter, milk, seasoning, black pepper and garlic powder. (Add more broth if needed) Pour mixture into greased baking dish/pan. Bake in 375 degrees oven for 45 minutes, until golden brown.

Giblet Gravy

1 c chopped giblets, cooked

2 c chicken broth

1 - 10 oz can cream of chicken soup

2 Tbsp flour mixed w/ ½ c water to create paste

½ pkg brown gravy

1 chopped hard-boiled egg

¼ tsp Creole seasoning

¼ tsp garlic powder

¼ tsp black pepper

In pot, add all ingredients together and bring to boil. Reduce heat. Cover and simmer for 15 minutes.

Chicken Pot Pie

1-12 oz can chicken
1-10 oz can cream of chicken soup
1 c chicken broth
1-15 oz can of mixed vegetables
2 Tbsp butter
1 Tbsp flour
1 tsp Creole seasoning
1½ tsp Cajun seasoning
½ tsp garlic powder
¼ tsp black pepper

Pie Crust

2 - 9 in deep dish pie crust
1 egg white
1 Tbsp water

Preheat oven to 375 degrees. Mix egg white and water together. Baste bottom of pie crust with egg white mixture. Pre-bake 1 pie crust at 375 degrees for 10 minutes. Remove crust from oven. Mix together Chicken Pot Pie ingredients. Pour into crust. Top pie with remaining crust. Trim and seal edges. Cut small slits into top crust. Brush crust with softened butter. Cover edges with foil to prevent edges from burning. Bake at 375 degrees for 40 minutes or until filling is bubbly.

Chicken and Dumplings

1 whole chicken, in parts
4 c chicken broth
½ c butter
1 c chopped onions
1 c chopped bell peppers
2 chopped garlic cloves
2 chopped green onions
2 tsp Creole seasoning
½ tsp garlic powder
¼ tsp black pepper
1 bay leaf
1 can favorite biscuits

In large pot add all ingredients together, except biscuits. Bring to boil. Cover and reduce heat. Cook until chicken is tender. Add biscuits pieces. Stir gently between adding biscuits. Cook for approx. 15 minutes.

Cabbage

1 cabbage (chopped)
1 lb chopped smoked sausage
1 diced potato
1 c chopped onions
1c chopped bell peppers
2 chopped garlic cloves
2 chopped green onions
2 tsp Creole seasoning
¼ tsp seasoning salt
½ tsp garlic powder
¼ tsp black pepper
1 bay leaf
1 Tbsp vegetable oil
3 c chicken broth

Add vegetable oil to pot. Add smoked sausage and sear. Add and sauté onions, bell peppers, garlic, green onions and bay leaf. Add seasonings, garlic powder, and black pepper. Add cabbage, potatoes and chicken broth. Cook 20-25 minutes on medium heat or until tender.

Stuffed Bell Peppers

6 green peppers
½ lb ground beef
½ c chopped onions
¼ c bell pepper
½ c chopped green onions
2 chopped garlic gloves
½ c butter
2 c cooked rice
season to taste

Wash bell peppers. Cut off bell peppers tops and remove insides. Brown ground beef and drain. Add butter, onions, bell pepper, green onions and garlic cloves. Cook approx. 10 minutes. Add cooked rice. Season to taste. Stuff bell peppers. Bake at 350 degrees for 25-30 minutes.

Squash Casserole

3-4 sliced squash, cooked and drained
1 lg chopped onion
1 sm chopped bell pepper
2 Tbsp butter
1 - 15 oz can cream corn
1 - 10 oz can cream mushroom soup
1 - 6 oz pkg Mexican cornbread, cooked
1 c shredded cheese
1 tsp Creole seasoning
½ tsp garlic powder
¼ tsp black pepper

Sauté onions and bell peppers in butter. Add cooked squash, cream corn and cream of mushroom soup. Add cooked cornbread. Add seasonings. Pour into greased casserole dish. Top with cheese. Bake at 350 degrees for 30 minutes.

Candied Yams

2 med size sweet potatoes, peeled and sliced
1 Tbsp butter
1½ c sugar
½ tsp nutmeg
½ tsp ginger
¼ tsp cinnamon
2 tsp vanilla extract
½ tsp lemon extract
2 c water

Boil sweet potatoes until tender. Drain. Place sweet potatoes in large skillet, add butter, water, sugar, nutmeg, ginger, cinnamon, vanilla and lemon extract. Bring to boil and reduce heat. Boil on medium heat for about 20 minutes, stir occasionally, or until a sugary candy coating forms. Remove from heat. Serve.

Bread Pudding

4 jumbo biscuits, baked
2 c milk
1 c sugar
½ c flour
2 tps vanilla extract
¼ tsp lemon extract
½ tsp nutmeg
¼ tsp ginger
¼ tsp cinnamon
1 c raisins

Heat oven to 375 degrees. In large bowl, crumble biscuits. In medium bowl, mix sugar, flour, milk, vanilla extract, lemon extract and spices. Toss raisins in flour, then dust off excess. Add raisins. Pour mixture into large bowl with biscuits, mix. Pour into greased baking pan. Bake 35 to 45 minutes or until golden brown.

Rum Sauce

¼ c rum
1 c confectioners sugar
½ c milk
½ teaspoon vanilla extracts
½ teaspoon almond extracts

In a small sauce pan, add rum and place over a low heat. Gradually add confectioners sugar and milk, stir, remove from heat. Stir in extracts. Pour sauce over bread pudding portions prior to serving.

Banana Pudding

½ c sugar

3 Tbsp cornstarch

1- 5 oz vanilla or banana (cook) pudding, not instant

7 oz - condense milk

2 ½ c milk

1 ½ tsp vanilla

1 tsp banana extract

¼ tsp lemon extract

1 box vanilla wafers

3 lg bananas, sliced

½ c cool whip (Optional)

Place vanilla wafers in bottom of dish. Top with bananas. Repeat layers.

Mix sugar, cornstarch and pudding in a saucepan. Add milk and condense milk, stir. Bring to boil constantly stirring for 5 minutes. Remove from heat. (If pudding has lumps, sift.) Add vanilla, banana, lemon and vanilla extract. Allow to cool. (If you prefer a lighter, fluffy pudding, fold in cool whip.)

Cover vanilla wafers and bananas with pudding. Chill. Serve.

Optional: Add meringue

Beat 2 egg whites until peaks form. Add ¼ c sugar and ½ tsp vanilla extract. Beat until peaks form. Spread on banana pudding. Bake at 450 degrees for 5 minutes or until golden brown.

Banana Bread

2 ripe bananas, mashed
½ c butter
1¼ c sugar
1 egg
2 tsp vanilla extract
2 c all-purpose flour
2 tsp baking powder
¼ tsp baking soda
¼ tsp salt
½ c milk
1 c chopped walnuts (optional)
1 c raisins (optional)

Mix butter, egg, and sugar in large bowl. Add vanilla extract. Add mashed bananas. Add flour, baking powder, baking soda, salt, chopped nuts (optional) and raisins (optional). Mix well. Pour into greased baking pan. Bake at 350 degrees for 30-35 minutes or until toothpick inserted comes out clean.

Peach Pie

1 - 29 oz can peaches
¾ c sugar
¼ c brown sugar
¼ c flour
1 Tbsp Butter
¼ tsp lemon extract
1 tsp vanilla extract
½ tsp nutmeg
¼ tsp cinnamon
¼ tsp ginger
2 - 10 in deep dish pie crust
Topping: butter, sugar and cinnamon

Preheat oven to 375 degrees.
Add all ingredients in medium pot. Bring to a boil. Remove from heat. Pour ingredients into pie crusts. Top with remaining pie crust. Spread butter over crust. Sprinkle with cinnamon and sugar. Bake at 375 degrees, 40 minutes or until juice starts bubbling around edges.

Tip: If top of pie starts to brown too fast, lay a piece of foil on top of pie. Remove foil approximately 10 minutes before pie is ready and continue baking. Lay a piece of foil in oven under pie for excess drippings from pie during cooking.

Homemade Pie Crust

3 c flour
2 c cold butter
¼ c vegetable shortening
1 tsp salt
1 Tbsp sugar
2 tsp vinegar
½ - ¾ c ice cold water

In large bowl add flour. Mix flour, butter and shortening until crumbs are formed. Add salt, sugar, vinegar and water. Gently combine together. Form a ball. Cut in half. Wrap in plastic wrap. Chill 30 minutes. Sprinkle flour on counter. Roll dough approx. ¼ inch thick.

Strawberry Pie

3 qt fresh strawberries, divided
1 ¾ c sugar
6 Tbsp cornstarch
3 oz raspberry gelatin
1 c water
2 - 10 in deep dish graham cracker or
pastry crust, slightly baked
8 oz whipped topping
½ tsp vanilla extract
Food coloring (optional)

Wash and slice 2 qts strawberries. Combine 1½ sugar, cornstarch, and gelatin. Add water. Bring to boil and cook 5 minutes stirring constantly. Add drop of food coloring (optional). Cool. Pour berry mix over strawberries and stir. Fill pie crust.

Topping
Add ¼ c sugar and ½ tsp vanilla to whipped topping, mix. Cover pie with whipped topping. Garnish with remaining whole strawberries. Chill. Serve.

Tip: Before baking crust, mix 1 beaten egg white and 1 Tbsp water together. Brush crust with mixture. Bake at 350 degrees 10 minutes or until golden brown.

Cream Cheese Pecan Pie

Cream Cheese Mixture

2 - 10 in graham cracker crust
1 - 8 oz pkg softened cream cheese
½ c sugar
1 egg
2 tsp vanilla extract
2 c chopped pecans

Pecan Pie Filling

5 eggs
2 c corn syrup
¼ c sugar
2 tsp vanilla extract

Cream Cheese Mixture: Mix together cream cheese, sugar, egg, and vanilla extract. Spread into graham cracker crust. Top with pecans.

Preheat oven to 375 degrees.

Pecan Pie Filling: Mix together 5 eggs, 2 c corn syrup, ¼ c sugar and 2 tsp vanilla extract. Pour over pecans. Bake at 375 for 35-40 minutes.

Creamy Lemon Pie

Lemon Pie Filling

1 - 9 in graham cracker crust
1 - 14 oz can condense milk
½ c whipped topping
½ tsp lemon extract
3 lemons, squeeze and strain juice

Meringue

2 egg whites
¼ c sugar
½ tsp lemon extract

Lemon Pie Filling:

In medium bowl mix condense milk, whipped topping, lemon juice, and lemon extract. Pour into crust.

Meringue:

Beat egg whites in a medium bowl until peaks form. Add sugar and lemon extract. Spread on pie. Bake at 450 degrees for 5 minutes or until golden brown. Chill. Serve.

Perfect Sweet Potato Pie

3 med sweet potatoes, cooked
½ c butter
1 ½ c sugar
2 Tbsp flour
¼ tsp salt
2 tsp baking powder
½ tsp nutmeg
½ tsp ginger
½ tsp all spice
2 tsp vanilla extract
½ tsp lemon extract
2 eggs, beaten
¾ c milk
2 - 9 in unbaked pie crusts

Pre-bake pie crust at 375 degrees for 10 minutes. Mix sweet potatoes and butter. Add sugar, flour, salt, baking powder and spices. Add eggs and milk. Add vanilla and lemon extract. Pour into crusts. Bake at 375 degrees for 45-50 minutes or until knife comes out clean.

Buttermilk Pie

2 c sugar
½ c butter, softened
3 eggs, slightly beaten
1 c buttermilk
2 tsp vanilla extract
1 tsp almond extract
4 Tbsp flour
1 - 9 in pie crust

Preheat oven to 350 degrees. Pre-bake pie crust for 10 minutes. Mix together sugar and butter. Add eggs, buttermilk, vanilla, almond extract and flour. Pour into pie crust. Bake at 350 degrees for 1 hour or until knife comes out clean.

Strawberry Cake

1 box white or strawberry cake mix
1 box strawberry gelatin
3 eggs
1 tsp baking powder
½ c cooking oil
½ c frozen strawberries
½ c milk
¾ box confectioners sugar
1tsp vanilla extract

Mix cake mix, gelatin, baking powder, oil, and milk. Add eggs, beating one at a time. Add strawberries. Bake at 350 degrees for 30-35 minutes.

Icing

Add ¾ box confectioners sugar, vanilla extract and remaining strawberries. Mix ingredients. Pour on cake.

Honey Bun Cake

1 box butter cake mix
8 oz sour cream
1 tsp vanilla extract
3 eggs
½ c butter
¾ c milk

Brown Sugar Mix

1 c brown sugar
2 tsp cinnamon
1 tsp flour
(don't forget to mix flour with brown sugar
and cinnamon, very important)

In a large bowl mix butter cake mix, sour cream, vanilla extract, eggs, butter and milk together.

In small bowl mix brown sugar, cinnamon and flour together.

Pour ½ batter in pan, spread ½ brown sugar mix over batter. Pour remaining batter in pan, spread remaining brown sugar mix over batter. Bake at 350 degrees for 30-35 minutes or until inserted toothpick comes out clean. Cool. Pour cream cheese icing over cake.

Cream Cheese Icing

8 oz cream cheese, room temperature
¼ c butter, room temperature
1/8 c milk
2 tsp vanilla extract
½ tsp lemon extract
2 c confectioners sugar

Beat cream cheese and butter. Add milk and vanilla extract. Gradually, beat in confectioners sugar. Add more confectioners sugar to thicken or milk to thin icing.

7up Cake

1 c butter, room temperature
3 c sugar
4 eggs, room temperature
3 c flour (sifted)
2 tsp baking powder
¼ tsp baking soda
¼ tsp salt
2 tsp lemon extract
2 tsp vanilla extract
2tsp almond extract
1¼ c 7up

Cream butter and sugar together. Add eggs one at a time. Beat until fluffy. Add extracts. Add baking powder, baking soda and flour. Add 7up. Grease and flour bundt pan. Pour batter in pan. (Do not turn oven on until cake is oven.) Bake at 325 degrees for 1 hour and 10 minutes or until toothpick inserted comes out clean.

Rum Cake

1 pkg butter cake mix
1 c flour
½ c sugar
1 tsp baking powder
4 eggs
½ c milk
½ c vegetable oil
½ c rum
2 tsp vanilla extract

Mix together cake mix, flour, sugar, baking powder, eggs, milk, vegetable oil, rum and vanilla extract. Pour into greased and floured bundt pan. Bake at 325 degrees for 50 minutes-1 hour or until toothpick inserted comes out clean.

Glaze

¼ c butter
¼ c milk
1 c sugar
½ c rum
1 tsp vanilla extract

Add butter, milk and sugar to saucepan. Boil 5 minutes. Remove from heat and add rum and vanilla. Pour over cake.

Pound Cake

1 c butter, room temperature

3 c sugar

4 eggs, room temperature

1 tsp lemon extract

1 tsp almond extract

1 tsp vanilla extract

3 c all-purpose flour

1 tsp baking powder

¼ tsp baking soda

¼ tsp salt

1 c buttermilk

Grease and flour bundt/cake pan. Mix butter and sugar together until fluffy. Add eggs and flavor extracts. Add flour, baking powder, baking soda and salt. Add milk. Mix together ingredients. Pour mixture into greased and floured pan. (Do not turn on oven until it's time to bake cake.) Bake at 350 degrees for 60 minutes or until inserted toothpick comes out clean.

Cream Cheese Glaze

½ c cream cheese
¼ c softened butter
2 tsp vanilla extract
¼ tsp almond extract
¼ tsp lemon extract
1½ c confectioners sugar
¼ c milk

Mix all ingredients together until smooth. Add more confectioners sugar to thicken or milk to thin icing. Pour over cake.

Soft Drop Tea Cakes

1 c butter

2 ½ c sugar

3 eggs

4 c flour

1 tsp baking powder

1 tsp baking soda

¼ tsp salt (optional)

½ c buttermilk

1 tsp vanilla extract

1 tsp almond extract

1 tsp butter extract

½ tsp ginger

1 tsp nutmeg

Preheat oven to 375. Cream butter and sugar together. Add eggs one at a time. Add extracts, ginger and nutmeg. Add baking powder, baking soda, salt and flour. Add buttermilk. Spoon onto ungreased cookie sheets. Bake at 375 for 10 minutes.

Sugar Cookies

1 c butter, softened
2 c sugar
2 eggs
2 tsp vanilla extract
1 tsp almond extract
3c flour
1tsp baking powder
¼ tsp salt

Mix together butter and sugar. Add eggs and beat until creamy. Add vanilla and almond extract. Add flour, baking powder, and salt. Mix well. Refrigerate 1 hour. Spoon onto ungreased cookie sheet. Bake at 400 degrees for 10 -12 minutes.

Peanut Butter Cookies

2 c creamy peanut butter
1 c butter
1 c sugar
1 brown sugar
2 eggs
1 tsp baking powder
1 tsp baking soda
¼ tsp salt
2 tsp vanilla extract
1 tsp almond extract
¼ tsp lemon extract
2½ c all-purpose flour

Mix together peanut butter and butter. Add sugar. Add eggs. Add extracts. Add baking powder, baking soda and salt. Mix in flour. Combine ingredients. Drop on ungreased cookie sheets. Bake at 375 for 8-10 minutes or until golden brown.

Fruit Salad

1 cubed cantaloupe
1 cubed pineapple
2 c sliced strawberries
1 cubed small watermelon
2 c green grapes
2 c red grapes
½ c pineapple juice
¼ c orange juice
½ c sugar
1 c water

Toss all fruit together. Add sugar and water to saucepan. Boil for 5 minutes. Pour syrup mixture over fruit. Mix pineapple juice and orange juice together and pour on fruit. Toss. Chill and serve.

Strawberry Lemonade

2 pkg strawberry flavored drink mix
1 c lemonade drink mix
1 ½ c sugar
1 - 14 oz pkg frozen strawberries
2 sliced lemons
1 gallon water

Mix ingredients together. Serve.

Happy Punch

1 - 12 oz c frozen orange juice
1 - 12 oz c frozen pineapple juice
1 - 10 oz c favorite frozen daiquiri mix
6 c 7up
3 c water
½ c rum (Optional)

Mix all ingredients together. Add ice. Serve.

Simple Punch

1 liter 7up
1 liter Gingerale
1 - 12 oz c frozen pineapple juice

Mix all ingredients together. Add ice. Serve.

About the Author

Phyllis Taylor has been experimenting in the kitchen with recipes since she was eight years old. She is the eleventh of twelve siblings. She grew up watching her parents, sisters, and brothers cook. One of her siblings decided to go into the restaurant business, Taylor's Catering and Restaurant. When Phyllis would visit her grandmother during her childhood, she would give her flour, butter, and sugar so that she could bake and continue to experiment as much as she desired. After years of experimenting with recipes, she is passing some of her favorite recipes on. Phyllis's Favorite Recipes has been created with a labor of love. Every recipe tastes great . . . simply delicious. You will want to cook and eat every item in Phyllis's Favorite Recipes cookbook over and over and share it with others. Enjoy!